cloverleaf books™

Money Basics

Kyle Keeps Track of Cash

Lisa Bullard

illustrated by Mike Byrne

M MILLBROOK PRESS · MINNEAPOLIS

For Alex —L.B.
For Nat —M.B.

Millbrook Press
A division of Lerner Publishing Group, Inc.
241 First Avenue North
Minneapolis, MN 55401 USA

For reading levels and more information,
look up this title at www.lernerbooks.com.

Main body text set in Slappy Inline 18/28.
Typeface provided by T26.

Library of Congress Cataloging-in-Publication Data

Bullard, Lisa.
    Kyle keeps track of cash / by Lisa Bullard ; illustrated by
Mike Byrne.
        p.   cm. — (Cloverleaf books™ — Money basics)
    Includes index.
    ISBN 978–1–4677–0762–6 (lib. bdg. : alk. paper)
    ISBN 978–1–4677–1694–9 (eb pdf)
    1. Money-making projects for children—Juvenile literature.
2. Money—Juvenile literature. I. Byrne, Mike, 1979– illustrator.
II. Title.
HF5392.B853 2014
331.702—dc23   2012048934

Manufactured in the United States of America
3-48709-12963-10/29/2019

TABLE OF CONTENTS

Chapter One

Our Club Is Going Camping

"Who wants to go camping?" asked Mr. Jackson. We all cheered.

"Great," he said. "Now, camping costs money." He wrote *budget* on the board. "We can make a budget to help us keep track of our money."

Budget

Expenses

Campground
Food
Water
Ice
Bug spray
Trash bags
Flashlights
+Gas for bus

$30 for each camper

He wrote *expenses* next. "Expenses are the things we spend our money on. We need to pay for our spot at the campground. We need supplies. Our expenses add up to **$30.00 for each camper**."

"I don't have **$30.00**," I said. "I just emptied my piggy bank."

"That's okay, Kyle," he said. "Budgets also track income. *Income* is the money we take in."

Do you have any income? It could be money you get for chores or an allowance. Include gift money too.

"Our club saves money in the bank downtown," said Mr. Jackson. "We spent some of that money to buy boxes of Cool Candy."

"Yum!" I said.

Where do you save your money?

"The candy isn't for you to eat," said Mr. Jackson. "You're going to sell it for income. Each camper gets ten boxes. You'll sell them for $3.00 each."

I ran out of fingers to count. But Keisha called out, "We'll each make $30.00!"

Chapter Two

Selling Candy

At home, I showed my family the candy. My brother ran to his room. He came back and put some money on the table.

"Cool Candy, please!" he said.

I found a notebook to do the math. "Quarters are worth 25¢. Eight quarters equals $2.00. Dimes are worth 10¢. Seven dimes is 70¢. Nickels equal 5¢. Five nickels is 25¢. Pennies are 1¢ each. Eight pennies make 8¢. You gave me $3.03. I owe you three pennies."

His mouth was already full.

How many quarters make $3.00?

The next day, Dad said he would take me out to
sell candy. I put all nine boxes in my backpack.
I added the notebook and the pencil.

Dad gave me ten **$1.00** bills. "Put this money in your wallet," he said. "You'll need it to make change. You can pay me back later."

Who is pictured on the $1.00 bill? Who is pictured on the $5.00 bill?

Mrs. Harding wanted two boxes. "They're $3.00 each," I said. "So that totals $7.00?" Dad shook his head. I tried again. "Two boxes is **$6.00!**" I said. Mrs. Harding gave me a $10.00 bill.
"That's **$10.00** minus **$6.00** equals **$4.00**." I counted four $1.00 bills into her hand.

Ms. Jennings bought one box. She gave me a $5.00 bill. I gave her back $2.00. Mr. Spire gave me two $1.00 bills and four quarters.

"All this candy's making me hungry," said Dad. "Time to go home for dinner."

Chapter Three

A Big Spender

Two days later, we tried selling again. But Ms. Clements doesn't eat candy. And Mr. Randall had already bought some from Keisha.

"If Keisha got here first, I'll never sell all my boxes!" I said.

Dad smiled. "I've got a great idea. Let's grab the bus and visit cousin Asheena."

Dad's idea *was* great. Asheena bought four boxes! "Maybe you can come over next Sunday and help me eat it?" she asked.

I smiled. "Thanks, Asheena!" She gave me a $20.00 bill from her purse. "Eight dollars back," I said.

Chapter Four

Camping, Here I Come!

Back home, Dad said, "Do I get any candy?"

"One last box for you!" I said. Dad paid me $3.00. I gave him back the $10.00 I owed him. Then I counted the rest of my money. I had one $20.00 bill and six $1.00 bills. I had twelve quarters, seven dimes, and five nickels. And I had five pennies.

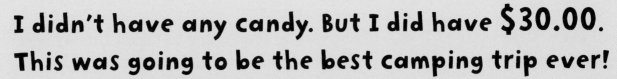

I didn't have any candy. But I did have $30.00.
This was going to be the best camping trip ever!

Once you've eaten it, candy is gone. What could you buy that lasts longer?

Play Store

Have you ever played store? It is a great way to learn how to count money and make change! You can buy play money at the dollar store. Or you can make pretend money using paper.

1) Put price tags on your toys, clothes, and snacks. Put half of the play money in a shoebox. Now your store is ready.

2) Invite a friend or someone in your family to shop in your store. Give them the rest of the play money. When they buy the items from your store, you can practice giving them the right amount of change.

3) Then turn things around. This time, you be the shopper. But give yourself only $10.00 to spend. Which things do you need the most when you have only a small amount of money? Do you need to make a budget? Pretend you have to take care of a family. Do you need to buy food and clothes, or do you need to buy toys?

GLOSSARY

allowance: money paid to a person, often a child, on a regular basis

bills: paper money

budget: a way to keep track of the money being taken in and the money being spent

chores: the everyday jobs that need to be done by a family

coins: pieces of metal, usually round and flat, that are used as money

expenses: things that money is spent on

income: money that is taken in, such as gifts or money earned

owed: needing to pay someone back

purse: a small bag used to carry things such as money

wallet: a small, flat case used to carry money

ANSWER KEY

page 11: Twelve

page 13: George Washington is on the $1.00 bill. Abraham Lincoln is on the $5.00 bill.

BOOKS

Larson, Jennifer S. *Do I Need It? Or Do I Want It? Making Budget Choices.*
Minneapolis: Lerner Publications Company, 2010.
Read more about making a budget and how to figure out if something is a need or a want.

Wells, Rosemary. *Bunny Money.* New York: Penguin, 1997.
Follow along as Ruby and Max go shopping for Grandma's birthday in this funny story.

Williams, Rozanne Lanczak. *The Coin Counting Book.* Watertown, MA: Charlesbridge, 2001.
Photographs and rhyming text will help you learn more about counting coins in this fun book.

WEBSITES

Counting Money
http://www.hbschool.com/activity/counting_money/
This online game helps you practice adding up how much a group of coins is worth.

H.I.P. Pocket Change
http://www.usmint.gov/kids/
Find games, animated money stories, coin news, and more at this site for kids from the U.S. Mint.

Learn about Money for Kids
http://kids.usa.gov/money/index.shtml
Watch a video showing how money is created, read about why saving money is important, and find links to more money-related activities.

LERNER SOURCE
Expand learning beyond the printed book. Download free, complementary educational resources for this book from our website, www.lernersource.com.